ACKNOWLEDGEMENTS
Thanks to Iain Ferguson, Esme Choonara, Kate Connelly,
Hannah Dee, Chris Nineham and Ian Birchall for their genuinely
helpful comments.

ABOUT THE AUTHOR
Mike Gonzalez is a senior lecturer in Hispanic Studies at Glasgow
University. He has written widely on the politics of Latin America
and his last book was *Che Guevara and the Cuban Revolution*
(Bookmarks Publications 2004). He is a regular contributor to the
International Socialism journal and is a member of the Socialist
Worker Platform within the Scottish Socialist Party.

INSIDE FRONT PHOTOGRAPH
The great Chartist meeting on Kennington Common, 10 April 1848.
The first photograph of a demonstration.

INSIDE BACK PHOTOGRAPH
National Guardsmen pose in front of a barricade in the Place
Vendôme, during the Paris Commune, March 1871.

PUBLISHED BY BOOKMARKS PUBLICATIONS 2006
ISBN: 1905192088
DESIGNED BY NOEL DOUGLAS (noel@noeldouglas.net)
PRINTED BY CAMBRIDGE PRINTING

A Rebel's Guide to
MARX

MIKE GONZALEZ

★1: THE BIRTH OF AN 'IMPUDENT' REBEL

Karl Marx was a revolutionary. Towards the end of his life he sometimes said that, when he looked at the people who called themselves Marxists, he wondered whether he was a Marxist himself. There have been many occasions since Marx's death in 1883 when his name has been used to justify tyranny and exploitation — claims that flew in the face of everything he believed. And yet the *Communist Manifesto* he wrote with his lifelong collaborator Friedrich Engels was a surprise bestseller at the end of the 1990s, and at the beginning of the 21st century Marx topped a vote by BBC radio listeners as to who was the greatest philosopher of all time.

But it is not entirely right to describe him as a philosopher. After all Marx himself said that "the philosophers have only *interpreted* the world; the point, however, is to *change* it." This famous sentence marks a key moment in Marx's own development, the moment when the philosopher began to change into the revolutionary thinker.

Karl Marx was born in 1818, the son of a well-off Jewish family in Trier, in the Rhineland in Germany. Napoleon's armies had briefly occupied the town at the turn of the century, before it was returned to the control of a Prussian state ruled by an absolute monarchy. Bonaparte's stay in the town was short, but he left behind some of the ideas about freedom and change that the French Revolution had introduced.

Marx's father, Hirschel, was known to make occasional public comments on the need for a properly representative political system, as well as denouncing the discrimination suffered by Jews in Prussia. Heinrich (he had converted in the meantime from Judaism to Protestantism and changed his name) was no revolutionary — but neither was he immune to the new air that was blowing across Europe. The young Karl cannot fail to have absorbed some of his father's liberal ideas.

His father insisted that Karl study law — a useful profession! So in 1835, at the age of 17, Marx began his legal studies at the University of Bonn. But he was more interested in poetry, wine and philosophy (not necessarily in that order). That was partly a result of the influence of Ludwig von Westphalen, a wealthy friend of the family, who quoted Shakespeare and the Greek poets to young Karl. In 1843 his daughter, Jenny, would become Marx's wife and lifelong companion.

Marx's enthusiasm for philosophy was not just an academic preference. At the time when he was a student, philosophical debates were an opportunity to engage with questions about society, history and the development of human possibility. One outstanding writer overshadowed these passionate discussions — Hegel. He had been an enthusiastic supporter of the French Revolution; he had believed it would introduce the era when reason would begin to shape human affairs.

But by the time Marx encountered his ideas, Hegel had become a conservative thinker, convinced that god represented the highest rationality — and that the repressive and authoritarian Prussian state was its highest expression.

Marx brought his liberal ideas with him from Trier, so he was drawn to a group of young students dedicated to 'turning the master on his head' — the Young Hegelians. It was the earlier, revolutionary Hegel they identified with. They were atheists and liberals as well as bohemians and very good drinking companions, as Marx found when he moved to Berlin and joined their Doctors Club, where his beard and long hair were acceptable signs of a radical thinker.

The Young Hegelians and those around them were united in their hostility to the oppressive Prussian state; for them, the French Revolution of 1789 meant enlightenment and change, progressive ideas that could also transform a feudal Germany into a modern capitalist democracy.

Marx had already moved beyond the ideas he had absorbed during his father's gatherings at home. Yet it was his father's circle of progressive businessmen and their like who financed the *Rheinische Zeitung*, a progressive newspaper opposed to the still feudal Prussian state which the young Karl began to edit on his return to Trier in 1841.

Throughout Marx's life there was interplay between the development of his ideas and his experiences of political and social events. One early example concerned the abolition of the traditional right of peasants to gather wood in the forest. A new law defined it as theft because the wood was private property. The land barons and the new industrial classes who financed Marx's paper agreed that the law was entirely correct. So it seemed that a new capitalist economy based on private property would still provide no guarantees for the poor and the propertyless. By the same token, Marx realised that a state that existed to protect private property would offer no protection to the working classes.

For Marx, it was the first step towards making sense of society in terms of class. When he expressed some of his new ideas in the paper, the Prussian state censor found the paper's contents objectionable enough to stop its publication and get rid of its "increasingly impudent editor". Other progressive journals in Germany were suffering the same fate. Karl and Jenny moved to France shortly afterwards. Jenny's aristocratic family were not at all impressed by the penniless and increasingly radical journalist with whom Jenny had thrown in her lot. But it made little difference to either of them.

★2: MOVING ON: PARIS

A number of German exiles had gone to Paris, where the mantle of progressive ideas would now be assumed by a new journal — the *Deutsche Französische Jahrbücher*. In October, Marx invited the philosopher Ludwig Feuerbach to contribute an article on his key argument that ideas are the product of social being — that the beliefs which people have are shaped by the material and social circumstances in which they live. It was an enormously important insight that gave Marx the impetus to move on from Hegel and even beyond the Young Hegelians. The discussion was still fairly abstract, but it established that the transformation of the world was a material process. What mattered was the revolutionising of the actual conditions of life. Then new ideas and new possibilities would emerge in the course of that process.

The change in Marx's thinking was not just an intellectual leap. In France he came face to face with the reality of a mass working class in a developing industrial society, where communist and socialist ideas were already taking root — and not only among French workers, but also among the 40,000 or more German workers who had migrated there. Marx was moved by the "freshness and nobility" of these worker activists:

"It is among these 'barbarians' of our civilised society that history is preparing the practical element for the emancipation of mankind" (Karl Marx and Frederick Engels, Collected Works, vol 27 [*CW:27*], Moscow, 1975, p426).

The *Jahrbücher* lasted only one issue; the copies sent secretly to Germany had been intercepted and provoked the rage of government censors. Arrest warrants were issued for Marx and others, and the publishers took fright. Not for the first time and certainly not the last, Marx found himself with very few prospects and a rapidly disappearing household budget. In another sense, it was an unexpected opportunity to read and develop his ideas in often furious polemics with others in the movement. His notes from those times in Paris were not to be uncovered until much later, when they were published under the title *Economic and Philosophical Manuscripts of 1844* (or the *Paris Manuscripts* for short).

Marx was only 26. Yet these writings marked a great step forward in his understanding of the experience of work in a capitalist society. "Alienation" was not a term that Marx invented; but while earlier philosophers like Hegel saw it as a psychological condition or a feature of all human beings who lacked awareness, Marx located it in the material conditions of labour.

"The worker becomes an ever cheaper commodity the more commodities he creates. With the increasing value of the world of things proceeds in direct proportion the devaluation of the world of men...[the] realisation of labour appears as a loss of reality for the worker... The alienation of the worker in his product means not only that his labour becomes an object, an external existence, but

that it exists outside him...and the life that he has con-
ferred on it confronts him as something hostile and alien"
(Karl Marx, *Economic and Philosophical Manuscripts*,
Moscow, 1967, pp66-67).

This is the great paradox that is one of the founda-
tions of Marx's theories: human beings reshape the world
through their labour and create the means to free themselves in doing so. Yet under capitalism that process
distances the very people who do the producing from
that possibility of freedom, because the things that they
produce are taken from them and bought and sold as
objects — as *commodities* — over which the worker has no
control.

This is because of the social relations that prevail in
society — the class system which gives one class ownership of all that is produced, while the other, the majority
that produces the goods, possess nothing but their
capacity to labour, that the capitalist buys as if it were
just one more object. And what is produced is determined by the capitalist's desire to earn profits, not by
society's needs.

For the workers, then, the only means of overcoming
alienation is a practical fight against the capitalists. In
that very year of 1844 the struggles of the weavers of
Silesia, in Germany, provided Marx with a living example
of how workers could fight the system. Looking back to
his own country, Marx saw a class of manufacturers and
capitalists who were too weak to take on and defeat a
powerful state as their French equivalents had done in
1789. Only the working class, therefore, was capable of
delivering the challenge.

When some of his contemporaries argued that

German workers were not politically educated enough, Marx contemptuously replied that they had class consciousness in abundance — and quoted the battles waged by the weavers of Silesia as overwhelming evidence. Marx's passionate defence of the weavers marked the distance he had travelled from his colleagues of earlier years.

The study of the English economists who described the workings of the capitalist system of production had made an important contribution to Marx's new understanding. As he now began to speak of the "self-emancipation of the working class", that understanding was put at the service of the cause of revolution. History, he now knew, was driven by social forces pursuing economic ends — and not by any external force, be it god or reason.

In his critique of religion the philosopher Ludwig Feuerbach had also gone some way with Marx in the same direction; but Marx still had a further distance to go, to affirm that history was moved by human action, and that the transformation of human understanding came in the struggle to transform the material world and the conditions of production.

★3: TEN DAYS THAT SHOOK THE WORLD[1]

In 1844 Marx and his great collaborator Friedrich Engels met for the first time.[2] The son of an industrialist, Engels had already spent some time at his father's factory in Manchester in northern England and seen "the condition of the working classes" — their poverty and exploitation in the new factories, the misery of those who were driving the productive machine of industrial capitalism. And Engels was also in close contact with a growing mass movement — Chartism — which was beginning to organise working class resistance to the horrors of the new society.

The two young men (Engels was three years younger than Marx) already knew one another's writings before

---

1: The title of a famous book by John Reed about the Russian Revolution, Francis Wheen uses it with some wit to describe the first meeting between Marx and Engels in August 1844 (in Francis Wheen, *Karl Marx*, London, 1999, p76).
2: Strictly speaking it was the second; their paths had crossed briefly two years earlier, but they had barely spoken.

their August meeting in Paris. So this was a meeting of minds, the encounter of two revolutionaries who shared the conviction that their task was to develop a new communist worldview that could inform the revolutionary struggle of the working class.

But first there was a battle to win within the workers' movement, and especially with others who still retained some influence among German workers. *The Holy Family* is a long and sometimes obscure polemic directed at the Young Hegelians who had accompanied Marx on the earlier part of his journey. Now Marx and Engels defined themselves by their refusal to discuss ideas except in the context of politics.

"Ideas cannot carry out anything at all. In order to carry out ideas men are needed who can exert practical force" (quoted in August Nimtz, *Marx and Engels: Their Contribution to the Democratic Breakthrough*, Albany, 2000, p1).

From this moment on, Marx and Engels set out to build the organisation that could help to prepare for the revolution, what Engels called "the open war of the poor against the rich". Their activities did not escape the notice of the agents of the state in either France, where Marx still lived, or Germany, where Engels was speaking to political and workers' groups. The German language newspaper that Marx had been writing for, *Vorwärts,* was banned by the French authorities late in 1844; a few weeks later, in February 1845, Marx was expelled from France under pressure from the German state. Engels left Germany two months later, convinced that the order for his expulsion was already on its way.

The two revolutionaries met again in Brussels in

Belgium where some degree of political tolerance was still practised, although always under the surveillance of the political police. Marx was already drafting his *Theses on Feuerbach* and *The German Ideology*. Revolutions were made by real workers in concrete circumstances — and Engels could provide living evidence of both workers' struggles and the material conditions which Marx had already described in general in the *1844 Manuscripts*. Philosophy — approaching the world through ideas — was now replaced by revolutionary practice, the forging of the instruments that could bring about the end of capitalism and of alienation. Marxism was to be *the theory and practice of workers' revolution*.

Marx and Engels expressed this new vision in *The German Ideology*, in which communism was defined as "the doctrine of the conditions for the emancipation of the working class". The *Theses on Feuerbach*, in just three pages and 11 clear definitions, expressed with dramatic clarity the extraordinary break the two men were making. The Young Hegelians had argued that ideas and consciousness produced actions; that was why they had scorned the Silesian weavers' strike, because they were not yet "adequately conscious". Equally scornfully, Marx retorted that in changing the world human beings alter their thinking. The historical process, he said, was "a coincidence of the changing of self and the changing of circumstances".

"Life is not determined by consciousness, but consciousness by life" (Karl Marx and Frederick Engels, *The German Ideology*, London, 2004, p47).

It was also an insight that allowed Marx and Engels

to see how ideas are used to maintain class divisions. As they put it in *The German Ideology*:

"The ideas of the ruling class are in every epoch the ruling ideas, ie the class which is the ruling material force of society is at the same time its ruling intellectual force" (The *German Ideology*, p64).

What are presented as common sense, as universal, general truths are in fact what Marx called *ideology* — in other words, a way of seeing and making sense of the world from the point of view of one class. And that class controls not only the means of production, but also to a large extent the means of representation, of explanation. So, for example, nationalism suggests everyone in Britain has common interests, yet that only serves to veil deep-seated class conflicts at the heart of society. Ideology maintains social cohesion in the interests of the rulers for most of the time — concealing the interests from behind a mask of truth.

But this cannot happen without regular reinforcement. Everyday experience is constantly reminding people that they live in an unequal, unjust and divided world. Where once the churches propagated and reinforced the dominant ideology, in our society it falls to education on the one hand, and mass culture on the other to disseminate and reinforce such ideas. It is the clash between the experience of the exploited majority and the dominant ideology that produces the possibilities for new radical ideas gaining a hold. When workers are in open revolt against the system, millions can be won to new ideas that reflect their real interests.

Thus Marx arrived at his famous conclusion at the end of the *Theses on Feuerbach* that philosophers had to do more than just seeking to understand the world — they had to actively be part of struggles to transform it. This was the project to which Marx and Engels now dedicated their life and their energies.

In 1845 Marx accompanied Engels to England, where he met with Chartist leaders and others. It was at their insistence that a meeting of socialists living in London was called later that year; although neither Marx nor Engels could attend, it was a foretaste of things to come. Both men had emphasised the international character of capitalism, and argued the need for a working class response equally capable of crossing frontiers. Back in Brussels, they formed the Communist Correspondence Committees, forerunners of the International. Their purpose was to begin the process of "winning over the European proletariat to our convictions".

It could be argued that this was the germ of a new political party capable of relating directly to the struggles of the working class. Simple though that might seem, it is worth recalling that the conviction that revolutionaries should work in and with the working class whose liberation was the driving force of revolution was not shared by all those who called themselves communists. Not by any means!

At this stage, while Marx in particular never relented in his punishing writing schedule, it was questions of organisation that concerned both himself and Engels. While no one could necessarily predict the revolutionary events of 1848, there was already a change in the air as they set about bringing together the leaders of European socialism and clarifying the nature of their relationship to the working class movement. And they did this, as they so often did, in fierce debates with other tendencies within the movement, whose ideas would have led to very different kinds of organisational expression.

The ideas of Pierre-Joseph Proudhon, for example, expressed the convictions of artisans and skilled workers in arguing for the creation of associations that would operate outside the circuits of capital. But Proudhon was hostile to trade unions and "opposed to revolution". More important were the ideas of people like the radical tailor Wilhelm Weitling who, like the Frenchman Auguste Blanqui, remained unconvinced that the workers were yet ready to make revolution. Until they were, they argued, the task should fall to small conspiratorial groups to act on their behalf. Neither man seemed daunted by the failure of every attempt, by Blanqui and his followers among others, to successfully carry through this method of achieving social change.

For Marx and Engels, however, these ideas were a significant obstacle to the construction of a revolutionary organisation along the model of Chartism — a mass organisation of workers.

By late 1846 their ideas were winning new supporters, especially in the London-based League of the Just which was more open to Chartist influence than the other European branches of the group. There had been some suspicion of the "continental intellectuals" who seemed so dominant in Europe; but for Marx and Engels the issue now was the creation of a "party", or at least some common form of organisation. That would be the way in which their ideas would win acceptance. They agitated from Brussels for regular meetings of the Correspondence Committees and began to discuss issues of strategy and tactics: how should German communists relate to the liberal reformers, for example. This activity was the most telling answer to the accusation that Marx and Engels were simply acting as intellectuals.

As the atmosphere in Germany grew increasingly tense, and as the Chartist movement in England continued to grow, the two men were immersed in questions of political organisation — and their writings were contributions to that general task.

The London branch of the League of the Just now called for an international meeting in London on 1 May 1847. Marx and Engels had not been consulted over the call, but an envoy was sent to Brussels to convince them to join the League and attend the May gathering. It was the clearest evidence of their growing political authority within the movement.

In the event, the meeting took place early in June 1847; it became the first Congress of the newly named Communist League, which defined itself in its opening address "by our attack on the existing social order and on private property, by wanting community of property". And it adopted as its slogan "Working men of all countries, unite!" Only Engels and their close collaborator William Wolff could attend the meeting; Marx remained in Brussels. Yet the influence of the "Marx-Engels party" was already obvious, and would become more so as the second Congress of the League approached in November that year. For the aims of the League were becoming increasingly clear. As Engels put it:

"Communism is not a doctrine but a movement; it proceeds not from principles but from facts. [And] insofar as it is a theory, it is the theoretical expression of the position of the proletariat in this struggle...and the conditions for its liberation" (quoted in Nimtz, p52).

The November Congress brought together delegates from several countries that debated and argued for ten days over the kind of movement they were to build. Marx and Engels were both present and when agreement was finally reached, it was they who were charged with writing the manifesto of the new organisation. In Brussels Marx seemed to hesitate, or at least to delay writing — and this a man who could dash off hundreds of pages in no time at all. But the final deadline from London spurred him to action. Late in February 1848 *The Communist Manifesto*, written largely by Marx but bearing the names of both Marx and Engels, was sent to the printer. By the time it reached the street, just days later, Europe was in uproar.

★4: SWIMMING WITH THE REVOLUTIONARY TIDE

It was one of Marx and Engels' great achievements to have written the work that expressed so clearly the spirit of 1848 before it had made itself apparent. It is testimony to a political approach to the world that insisted on taking as its starting point the material reality of its time, as well as identifying the tensions and conflicts that lay, often barely visible, beneath the surface. They saw, in the famous opening sentence of the Manifesto that:

"A spectre is haunting Europe — the spectre of communism" (Karl Marx and Friedrich Engels, *The Communist Manifesto*, London, 2005, p7).

This is no ordinary political pamphlet: it is a passionate manifesto and a vision. To a 21st century reader, and all who read it in between, it sounded and sounds incredibly contemporary. It describes a world that we can instantly recognise today. Yet when the *Manifesto* was written it was a world still in its infancy. The industrial capitalism that Marx understood with such depth and insight was only in the first phase of its relentless progress. Marx and Engels had already unmasked the exploitation on which the whole system rested, the dehumanising impact of the drive to profit; yet they had done so before they could possibly have known how chillingly and powerfully accurate their words were to prove for the generations that came after them.

"The bourgeoisie cannot exist without constantly revolutionising the instruments of production and thereby the relations of production...and the whole relations of society...uninterrupted disturbance of all social conditions, everlasting uncertainty and agitation distinguish the bourgeois epoch from all previous ones. All fixed fast frozen relations...are swept away, all newformed ones become antiquated before they can ossify. All that is solid melts into air, all that is holy is profaned, and man is at last compelled to face with sober sense his real conditions of life and his relations with his kind.

"The need of a constantly expanding market for its products chases the bourgeoisie over the whole surface of the globe. It must nestle everywhere, settle everywhere, establish connections everywhere" (*The Communist Manifesto*, p12).

It takes an effort on the reader's part to remember that this was written before the search for oil absorbed the Middle East and transformed it into a battlefield for interests based half a world away, before Nike and Coca Cola stamped their mark on a thousand different cultures, before a stock market decision in London could destroy the lives of millions of people in poor countries.

What is so powerful here is not just the accuracy of the analysis, the description of the workings and impulses of a capitalist system. It is also the passionate exposure, the strength of the denunciation that underpins the words.

This, after all, is a *communist* manifesto — it recognises the aggressive dynamism of capitalism, but comes to bury the system, not to praise it. The question is, who will be the gravedigger?

The answer comes a little later in the work. As capitalism emerges from the old society the little workshop is absorbed into the great factories, small farmers and peasants become labourers in the intensified production system of modern farms that supply the growing cities, small traders are swept aside by the ever-growing units of national and international commerce — the BPs and the Halliburtons begin to form.

Workers drawn to the industries growing up in and around the cities find a new tyranny:

"Masses of labourers, crowded into the factory, are organised like soldiers. As privates of the industrial army they are placed under the command of a perfect hierarchy of officers and sergeants. Not only are they the slaves of the bourgeois class and of the bourgeois state; they are daily and hourly enslaved by the machine, by the overseer, and above all by the individual bourgeois manufacturer himself" (*The Communist Manifesto*, p13).

At first, pushed from pillar to post, bullied by the factory owners and threatened by the foremen, they do not resist in any organised way, though from time to time they will lash out in their rage and pain and smash the machines.

The irony, of course, is that the machine is not the enemy — only the purposes it serves. That, as Marx saw clearly, is the paradox: the more human beings are able to produce, the nearer they get to the *possibility* of freeing human beings from the slavery of labour. Yet under capitalism that possibility is snatched away; the machine, instead of liberating humanity, enslaves it more and more. But something else is also happening. The proletariat, the working class, is not only pulled towards the cities; it is also concentrated more and more as production becomes increasingly sophisticated and mechanised, allowing the bosses to extract ever more profit. This in turn gives the workers a growing collective strength that makes it possible for them to organise and confront the owners of the machine.

So for Marx, the working class was the agent of socialist revolution. That was not because he idealised workers in any way, nor thought them stronger or better fighters or somehow exempt from all the contradictory attitudes that arise in a capitalist society. Individual workers could be as selfish or sexist or cruel as anyone else. It was the unique position workers occupied in the new capitalist society that gave them both an interest in changing society and the potential power to do so. It is a class of people with no property and whose only weapon is their own collective power.

Marx wrote the *Communist Manifesto* in Brussels, much of it while sitting in the Blue Parrot Café in the central square — the Place de la Ville. It went to the printers in February 1848; as it hit the streets, word was arriving from France of barricades and fighting in the streets; the hated Guizot, the prime minister, resigned and the abdication of the king followed the very next day. Within weeks the insurrectionary spirit reached Berlin and another government fell to earth. Engels wrote excitedly, "The flames of the Tuileries and the Palais-Royal are the dawn of the proletariat... Everywhere the rule of the bourgeoisie will now come crashing down...Germany, we hope, will follow" (*CW*: 6, p356).

The authorities in Brussels took fright at the fires that were starting to burn across Europe and their tolerance of the Marxes came to an abrupt end. By March, Marx had been expelled to Paris, which he now announced to be the headquarters of the Communist League. Engels joined him there, and the two men began to prepare for a return to Germany. But there were ferocious arguments among the returning exiles, some of whom wanted to mount an armed expedition, a 'German legion', which Marx argued against with his usual vigour. For Marx, the key was to impel the organisation of a workers' movement, but within the broader movement for democracy. By April, Marx was back in Germany and preparing to publish a new daily newspaper in Cologne, the *Neue Rheinische Zeitung* (*NRZ*), as his instrument for intervening in the political debates within the revolutionary movement. At its height it sold 5,000 copies.

Four years earlier the first version of the paper had enjoyed the support of Germany's frustrated middle classes. This time they were more reluctant to back Marx's enterprise, which was so critical of the new institutions emerging after the fall of the old regime — like the new National Assembly. Workers' groups were being formed all over Germany, though their demands tended to focus either on solely immediate economic issues or on purely democratic demands. When the *Neue Rheinische Zeitung* came out in June, Marx and Engels saw it as the organising focus for communists.

What about the Communist League? Both Marx and Engels felt it was too small to have a major influence on events that were drawing thousands into public activity. In a time of upheaval and rapid change the key thing was to enjoy an influence over the larger movement rather than set the communists apart or even against it. Central to Marx's new worldview was the idea that great transformations of consciousness come in the context of material changes, but not automatically. New ideas will be adopted and absorbed only to the extent that they are present *within* the movement. That was the argument that spurred Marx's angry polemics with another leading German socialist, Gottschalk, who was popular among German workers but whose ideas encouraged the idea that workers should stand aside from the broader revolutionary movement.

The truth was that the German workers' movement was at a stage of its development where it was out to conquer democratic rights. In Britain, by contrast, the Chartist movement had reached a peak of influence, and Marx and Engels certainly saw it as the leading edge of the European workers' struggle. Equally, they were clear that united work with liberal elements must never mean conceding the political leadership of the movement to them.

Even as the *NRZ* was distributing its first numbers, events in Europe were once again leaping into a new phase. In France the democratic promises of the liberal government that had replaced the monarchy in February proved stillborn. The immediate gains of February now came under attack from the newly elected National Assembly with its right wing majority. In June the national workshops, which had provided guarantees of subsistence for urban workers, were abolished, leaving workers destitute. The masses took to the streets of Paris in protest. This time they were met with savage repression. When Marx denounced the behaviour of the cowardly French bourgeoisie, their German counterparts saw his condemnation as directed equally against them and withdrew their support for the paper.

In July, Germany also saw a relatively liberal government replaced by one more sympathetic to reaction; Marx and his paper were among the first targets for repression, and publication was prevented more than once in the months that followed. But as democratic rights came increasingly under threat, from Vienna to Berlin, Marx and his newspaper remained consistently vociferous champions of workers' rights. His authority was always thrown behind a strategy of building influence among workers — what he would later call "the revolution in permanence"; but he also actively argued against precipitate actions that would bring down the weight of reaction before the movement was ready to resist. It was a time, as Marx and Engels put it, of "revolutionary restraint". For it will have been obvious to them that the counter-revolution was preparing its backlash.

In Vienna the movement faced that repression in the streets; elsewhere in Germany mass demonstrations demanded support for their brothers and sisters in the Austrian capital. By October they were defeated, but it would be another two months before the counter-revolution could claim a victory in Berlin and in Germany as a whole with the coup that placed Frederick IV at the head of the Prussian state. Throughout the subsequent months Marx and Engels worked tirelessly, particularly through the newspaper, to rally the democratic forces, to forge alliances between workers and peasants, and, most importantly, to analyse and understand the movement in Germany as part of an international picture.

Despite a series of setbacks within Germany, the continuing struggles elsewhere in Europe encouraged Marx to feel optimistic about the revolutionary possibilities, and to support those organisations, like the Baden and Frankfurt provisional assemblies, which still mounted some resistance.

By mid-1849 the revolutionary movement was in retreat; the Hungarian rising was crushed by the troops of the Russian Tsar; in Germany reaction was clearly winning the day. On 16 May Marx was served with an order expelling him from Cologne and left for Paris the following day. Engels meanwhile joined the insurrectionary forces in Baden. Before they left, the final issue of the *Neue Rheinische Zeitung* was printed entirely in red ink.

"We had to surrender our fortress, but we withdrew with our arms and baggage, with band playing and flag flying...our last word always and everywhere will be: emancipation of the working class" (quoted in Nimtz, p101).

★5: LOOKING BACK, LOOKING FORWARD

Marx's reputation as an agitator and as the intellectual leader of the rising revolutionary movement meant that he was viewed with suspicion by the authorities wherever he went. Pressured to leave Paris, he and his family returned to London in August 1849. Soon afterwards his friend, comrade and companion Friedrich Engels joined him there. His nickname in their inner circle was "The General", a reflection of Engels' growing interest in the organisation of revolutionary insurrection after his experiences in Germany.

Although the revolutionary movements in Europe had suffered setbacks, both men were still optimistic about the prospects for new upsurges in Germany and France. The Marx family, as Jenny's correspondence poignantly shows, were in dire economic straits — what few funds they had were perhaps recklessly spent on aiding political comrades fleeing from Germany and in setting up another journal, whose first of five numbers was published in January 1850. Jenny arrived, pregnant, in a London grey with autumn in September; Marx was not uncaring, but he was still excited by the prospect of building a movement out of the extraordinary events of 1848-9.

In 1848 Marx and Engels had argued that the Communist League should be dissolved, and that it was more urgent for socialists to be involved in the broader movements emerging in the revolutions, and to fight for ideological influence within them. By early 1850 it was becoming clear that the key tasks were now different, and they argued just as forcefully that the League should be re-established. They also recognised that it would be a hugely important contribution to the next phase of creating a revolutionary organisation to learn from and understand the events which were still fresh in the memory of working class activists and socialists across Europe.

In three historic pieces of writing Marx analysed those events — the *Address* to a now reconstituted Communist League (of March and June 1850) and a series of essays published in their short-lived paper (between January and October), and later called *The Class Struggles in France 1848-1850*. The third account of these events, *The Eighteenth Brumaire of Louis Napoleon*, is probably Marx's historical writing at its most brilliant. But these were not just forensic interpretations offered by an objective and uninvolved observer. Marx, after all, had once again been elected as president of the Communist League's executive committee; his was an active and conscious contribution to the building of socialist organisation that would learn from and build on the 1848 revolutions. As he put it, "The revolution is dead — long live the revolution!"

What Marx drew from the experiences of 1848 were conclusions and insights that once again seem curiously contemporary. Yet unlike the many other commentators who published their versions of these events, Marx discussed the events from the point of view of the working class and in an effort to draw out the political and organisational consequences for future socialists.

The first conclusion was that in each case the revolution had initially brought important sections of the middle class into united action with the working class. That unity in action, however, had proved short-lived in both Germany and France. In both cases the bourgeoisie, which would be the main beneficiary of the introduction of parliamentary democracy — the chief immediate gain of the 1848 revolutions — now feared that the process might not stop there, and that the working class and its allies would drive things further and faster until they threatened the very existence of private property. So they turned against their erstwhile allies, and sought compromise and agreement in many cases with the old ruling classes they had so recently wanted to overthrow.

Given that the transformation of capitalist society will never be carried through to its conclusion by a class that has a stake in its preservation, it becomes imperative that the working class is able to continue with that transformation independently of yesterday's allies. It was in the bourgeoisie's interests to bring the revolution to a conclusion as rapidly as possible, "whereas it is in our interest, and it is our task, to make the revolution permanent". This idea of permanent revolution has become identified with the thinking of Leon Trotsky; but its origin is here, in Marx's reflections on the revolutionary experiences of 1848.

At the same time, Marx was engaged in another

fierce debate with the Blanquists who, having played an important role in the Paris insurrection, now reiterated emphatically their notion that the revolutionaries must act in secret. Marx and Engels were insistent on this point. It was critical that the working class should organise *independently* of the bourgeoisie, in the knowledge that sooner or later the bourgeoisie would attempt to call a halt to the movement. This could happen to the extent that the workers' movement had a clear understanding of its class interests, of those of the other classes in society, and of how revolution could come about. It was vital that at least a section of workers understood this in advance of the next revolutionary upsurge.

The building of a revolutionary party of the working class was now the task. Perhaps Marx was overly optimistic as to the immediate prospects of revolution at that point (as Engels recognised in a new preface to *The Class Struggles* written after Marx's death). But he was completely justified in his insistence that the task for revolutionaries was to build the party that could win the leadership of the revolutionary movement and carry it through to its conclusion. That conclusion, as he defined it here, was "the dictatorship of the proletariat".

Few of Marx's words have been subject to so much misunderstanding and misrepresentation as these. The word "dictatorship" has taken on such murderous meanings in a world that has known Nazism, Stalinism, and the endless varieties of tyranny that capitalism has thrown up in the last hundred years or so. When Marx used the word, it did not have the same meaning. In fact, he was talking about *all* forms of states, whatever the extent of democracy they possessed. Every state for Marx is an instrument of class rule.

In France and Germany the post-revolutionary state, many of whose ministers had briefly been allies of the working class in the struggle for democracy, turned against the workers with extreme savagery. What kind of state, Marx asked, would protect the interests of the majority — his answer was "the exclusive political rule of the working class with all the revolutionary changes in social conditions which are inseparable from it" (*CW*: 10, p298). Only such a state could defend the gains of the workers and supervise the transformation of social conditions that would guarantee them. At this stage Marx had only a general idea — a theory — to go on. The 1871 Paris Commune would reveal the reality.

In reflecting back on this exciting and world-changing time, Marx's careful analyses made a clear link between revolution and crisis within the economic system. Crises were not just the product of error or chance, but the result of capitalism's own inner conflicts. It was, he concluded, the absence of crisis — or to put it another way, the wave of prosperity and economic growth in England in the late 1840s that had deflated the revolutionary potential of Chartism. In France, on the other hand, the working class was not yet powerful or central enough to the economy to ensure its revolutionary potential.

For a revolutionary materialist like Marx, it was clear that "ideas do not change history" unless and until they are embodied, carried, by living social forces acting in material circumstances that make such change possible. Understanding what rhythms and impulses drove capitalism forward, and what circumstances produced crisis, was as fundamental a task for Marx as was the creation of working class organisations and the political preparation of its members.

★6: 'A NEW SCIENTIFIC OUTLOOK'

By the middle of 1850 it was becoming clear to Marx that revolution was no longer on the immediate agenda. European capitalism was moving into a period of growth and expansion but, as the persecution of the German communists in Cologne, after a failed assassination attempt against the emperor of Prussia would show, bourgeois democracy was only with some difficulty disentangling itself from the remnants of the old order.

Within the Communist League bitter arguments arose, for there were still many in the leadership of the organisation who were convinced that revolution remained a fairly imminent possibility, and that all that was needed was armed readiness and a great deal of conviction. In the aftermath of the 1848 movements, too, the arguments took on a nationalist tinge, as the German comrades insisted on the continuing radicalism of their national working class.

So for Marx and Engels there were two issues at stake; first, as they had so clearly written in the *Communist Manifesto*, the revolutionary movement of workers must be international in character. And secondly, that revolution must arise out of a conjunction of subjective (the consciousness of workers and the authority among them of revolutionary ideas) and objective (crises in the system) factors:

"A German national standpoint was substituted for the universal outlook of the *Manifesto*, and the national feelings of the German artisans were pandered to. The materialist standpoint of the *Manifesto* has given way to idealism. The revolution is not seen as the product of the realities of the situation but as a result of an effort of will. Whereas we say to the workers: you have 15, 20, 50 years of civil war to go through in order to alter the situation and to train yourselves for the exercise of power, [they say] we must take power at once, or else we may as well take to our beds" (quoted in Nimtz, pp143-144).

These were not easy times for Marx: his financial situation was dire, and he and his family had to move with some regularity; it must often have seemed that the selfless and constant support of Engels was the only thing that kept the Marx family back from the edge. At the end of the year their much-loved son Heinrich ("Fawkesy" Marx called him) died; six months later their live-in maid gave birth to a son, Freddy, certainly fathered by Marx — though he never acknowledged him. In fact Engels accepted paternity in order to protect his friend and colleague — neither his first sacrifice nor his last!

Marx now took up his regular place in the British Museum Reading Room. He had begun the extraordinarily ambitious project (for anyone but Marx) of defining and describing the general characteristics of the capitalist system as a whole. Some in the movement (generally speaking the ones who sat around late into the night planning insurrections) condemned this as a retreat from politics. Marx and Engels, however, were emphatically not withdrawing from political organisation — they never really abandoned the idea of party building, albeit in informal ways until the creation of the International in 1864.

Marx never withdrew from his polemics with other socialists, nor did he cease his regular production of pamphlets and articles. In the lull that succeeded their split from the Communist League, these debates and polemics were part of the process of building a new party.

But there is no doubt that at this stage Marx considered his studies and research into the capitalist system to be his main *political* task. It was not only a matter of knowing the enemy: the aim here was to understand the driving forces of the capitalist system and contradictions and tensions that its development produced. And given the inevitability of crisis, it was important to be able to anticipate, or even predict, when and where the cracks would appear. All this was part of the business of *preparing* the communists for the future battles in the class struggle.

The task he had set himself was to understand the way in which capitalism as a global system worked and developed through time — to uncover, as he put, its "laws of motion". But that was not all. The problem is that what appears on the surface might well not be what is actually driving the system from within. After all, Marx had analysed at length in his earlier work the way in which ideas and explanations of capitalism's mechanisms and laws often concealed or misrepresented what was really going on — this was what he meant by "ideology".

We know from our time, for example, how often economic decisions made by powerful actors in their own interests are presented to the world as natural phenomena. When those usually opaque statistics that seem to end every news bulletin describe the "movements of the market", or the rise and fall of this or that index, they seem often to be squeezed between accounts of disasters and the weather report, as if all of them belonged in the realm of things over which we could have no control. "[Bourgeois] economists express the relations of bourgeois production...as fixed, immutable, eternal categories" decided and determined by the interests of one class which stands in opposition to those who produce its wealth yet lack any power over the system and the way it functions (Karl Marx, *The Poverty of Philosophy*, Peking, 1978, pp97-98).

Marx's own youthful writing had described the experience of workers under capitalism — that alienation which produced the sense of powerlessness that most of them felt, and that profound feeling that the machines at which they worked had a life of their own. The question was what specific conditions of capitalism produced that relationship between the owners of capital and the producers of wealth; and what were the real driving forces that moved the system in its entirety forward, as opposed to the particular examples of this or that capitalist's behaviour and treatment of his workers. What was the global relationship between the class of capitalists and the class of workers in a capitalist system?

The answer, of course, was not to be found in abstract formulae — Marx was a materialist, after all. His approach, then, drew on the observation of the behaviour of real, living forces in real historical time; as in everything he did, the test of theory would be a practical one, explaining material reality and its development. And here, as in every historical movement, the process would be dialectical — producing contradictions and conflicts that could be resolved only by changing society. Those tensions expressed themselves in periodic crises under capitalism. It was vital that the revolutionary movement understood their nature, anticipated them and was organisationally prepared to exploit the opportunities they presented. So, for Marx, there was no doubt that this period of study and research was a direct and material contribution to that essentially political project.

"Our party was glad to have peace once more for study. It had the great advantage that its theoretical foundation was a new scientific outlook the elaboration of which kept it busy enough; for this reason alone it could never become as demoralised as the 'great men' of the exile" (*CW*: 16, pp470-471).

By "our party" Marx meant essentially himself and Engels. And it was just as well that despite the unpromising immediate prospects of struggle their spirits were not low — indeed Marx's resilience is especially remarkable bearing in mind the very dark days of poverty and insecurity that he and his family were going through, the endless moving from house to house, the frequent illness of all the family, including Karl and Jenny, and the death of another child, little Edgar. Only Engels' loyal and unselfish support kept them from going under.

Marx spent much of the next 20 years writing *Capital* — but the first part was not published until 1867 and it was not fully available to the public until after his death.

The first part to be published (in 1859) was his *Contribution to a Critique of Political Economy*.

★7: DEFINING THE BEAST

What were the core ideas that drove and shaped this extraordinary work? "Modern bourgeois society that has sprouted from the ruins of feudal society has not done away with class antagonism. It has but established new classes, new conditions of oppression, new forms of struggle in place of the old ones" (*The Communist Manifesto*, p8).

First, capitalism was a stage in a developing and changing history (and not, as some contemporary bourgeois theorists have claimed, the "end of history"!). It had emerged in specific historical conditions, and like all previous class societies was riven with internal contradictions. Second, the relentless impulse to create profit produced both technological advances and a search for means to make the worker increasingly productive. Hence that "constant revolutionising of production" that Marx had commented on so poetically in the *Communist Manifesto*. Third, the source of profit is labour itself, or rather the exploitation of labour. The contemporary world tends to see exploitation as a moral issue — as an abuse of power. Marx used the term in a more specific and technical sense — to describe that relationship between capital and labour in which capital seeks to squeeze from the labourer greater and greater amounts of value over and above what it costs to keep the labourer functioning — in other words, surplus value.

So, for Marx, capitalism was a class society, in which a small class owned the means of production (the *bourgeoisie*, he called them, though we might now call them the capitalist class) and the rest (the great majority) owned only their capacity to work (these were the *proletariat*, or working class).

Within each class there would be enormous variety — of gender, of race, of appearance and taste. There would be charitable bosses and tyrannical ones, racists and liberals, nationalists and cosmopolitans; among the workers some would be educated and others not, some skilled and some not, some black and others white, some men and some women. Yet they belonged to classes because of their relationship with society's resources and how they were organised. The bourgeoisie, all of them, acted as one to defend their ownership of society's wealth; more than that, they used their power and authority to organise social production for their benefit.

"Accumulate, Accumulate. That is Moses and the Prophets" (Karl Marx, *Capital*, vol I, Harmondsworth, 1976, p592).

With that simple phrase, Marx summed up what drives capitalism forward. Those who own the means of production belong to the same class, but they are also rivals competing to dominate the market and raise their level of profit. It is profit that drives the system. A capitalist is not just someone who owns the means of production; he or she is someone who uses those resources to earn more money and to steal a march on his or her competitors. Capitalism is a way of organising the economic system to make that possible.

That system of organisation (Marx called it a *mode of production*) is complex, of course. It requires not only a certain way of preparing production itself, but a range of other forms and structures to keep it going, from the means of getting people to and from work, and the education that will teach them how to use the new machinery, to the creation of a series of cultural instruments that will persuade those who must do the producing that this is the best of all possible worlds despite their poverty. Marx analysed and discussed all these aspects.

But at the heart of it all was production. How did the capitalists earn their profits? They invested their money, bought the machinery, employed people and decided what and how to produce. But the actual creation of things was done by workers who were paid a wage to work at machines. In Marx's day the numbers of people doing just that were growing all the time. He could certainly have imagined the vast factories of the 20th century where thousands produced goods along vast production lines.

Then, as now, production is a very elaborate process in which all sorts of people take part. The cotton mills of the 19th century used cotton picked by slave labour in India and Egypt; vast numbers of people were involved in getting it to Lancashire. Others (fewer then than now) fed, educated and nursed the mill hands. Since then we have created armies of people to deal with the casualties of an increasingly brutal and inhuman system. What united and unites all these people at different points in the chain of production — from call centre operators to social workers to bus drivers — is their relationship with that system. They sell their labour-power for a wage to those who own the means of production.

The key to capitalist production, however, was the fact that the workers produced far more than they received back in wages; the difference between the worth of what they produced and the money they received in their wage packet — the surplus value — went into the pockets of the capitalists.

The bosses always argued, of course, that it was legitimate for them to take that money because they needed to reinvest and to be compensated for the "risks" they took in investing their money. But when the investment fails and workers lose their jobs, the managers and directors are richly recompensed and, unlike their workers, protected from the effects of their "risk-taking".

In fact, when they have renewed the machines and paid off the bank, what is left is profit, part of which goes towards the maintenance of the life style of the bourgeois. But part of it is also used to invest in new and better machinery that will enable workers to produce yet more surplus value, and give the investor an advantage over the competition. Yet presumably every capitalist is doing the same thing — what is it that gives one the edge over another? The answer is simple enough: the capitalist who manages to squeeze more production from the workers gets ahead.

But as each worker is coupled to more and more machinery, the very source of profit — the living labour of the worker — diminishes as a proportion of the total production process. This leads to a tendency for the *rate* of profit to decline, even if the total volume of profit is increasing. This represents a serious threat to capitalism in the long term.

So capitalist production is driven by the relentless, desperate need to accumulate profits at the expense of other capitalists. Accumulation and competition are the watchwords. And if the worker in one factory produces more than the worker in the next door plant for the same wages, then that factory's profits will rise. In practice this has meant laying hold of more and more of the earth's resources — consuming and destroying them — in that race for the market. Forests are felled, oil and gas are gouged out of the earth, fossil fuels are burned, agriculture is intensified, and more and more land is exhausted in the process. Yet the factories of today — once they were only in Europe and North America, today they are also in China, or Korea, or Mexico — are using up the resources of tomorrow.

Why can't they see it — why does George Bush refuse to recognise what is obvious to millions? In the constant race to compete the capitalist does not stop to think ahead — at least not beyond tomorrow — because all the rest are thinking the same way. It's one of the ironies of the impulse that Marx identified in capitalism — that in the long term it is globally destructive. But Halliburton and General Motors are not concerned about next year; the books have to show a profit today. That is Moses and the Prophets!

There was one further key question to ask — who were these goods produced *for*? In a society where production answered the needs of people, the decision as to what to produce would be determined by those needs — the factories would produce food for the hungry, ambulances for the sick. Yet it is perfectly obvious that some other consideration dominates under capitalism — so that a shortage of ambulances is combined with a huge surplus of arms, where millions go hungry for lack of staple foods while unimaginable quantities of unnecessary and unwanted foods are produced and, as likely as not, thrown away. That is because commodities are bought and sold in a market; there is no direct relationship between the producer and the consumer. And the decisions as to what is produced are made exclusively in terms of what produces profit.

Another consequence of production for the market is that there is no overall attempt to coordinate production with society's needs under capitalism. As Marx put it, the despotism of the factory is matched by its opposite, anarchy in the economy as a whole. Planning takes place inside the individual firm but overall the system is planless. It is this that makes instability, crisis, boom and slump inherent in the very nature of capitalism as an economic system, and not merely accidental features as many of its apologists like to claim. Capitalism is then, in its very nature, a system based on struggle, conflict and contradiction.

So we are left with a paradox. On the one hand capitalism is constantly evolving ways of making production more "efficient", moving constantly in search of cheap labour, developing technologies to do the work of many, fighting to hold down the price of raw materials. And yet on the other hand many workers today are spending more hours than ever in their workplace, and it seems that very soon they will be forced to add years to their working life as big capital claws back the pensions that they once reluctantly promised. So although capitalism has generated the potential to provide food, shelter and healthcare to the world's population, the nature of the system means that billions go without these basic necessities. What should represent the liberation of human beings from labour actually has the reverse effect *under capitalism*.

★8: CRISIS AND OPPORTUNITY

Marx looked back on 1848 as a time of capitalist crisis that had produced a revolutionary response. If the outcome had not been as he had hoped, it had demonstrated clearly both the power of the working class and the ruthlessness of their rulers. These were important lessons to carry into the next crisis — a crisis his studies revealed to be an inescapable consequence of capitalism's anarchic nature. And next time the working class movement should be ready.

In 1857 an economic crisis did occur. There was a certain irony in this for Marx, since just a year earlier Jenny had received a small inheritance that enabled them to pay their debts and move to better accommodation. In the event, the crash of '57 did not produce an upsurge of struggle. Yet there were stirrings of renewed activity, particularly in Europe. The working class was growing in numbers in France and Germany and new political expressions were filling the political space left by the demise of the most radical expression of working class organisation — Chartism.

In Britain in 1863 massive meetings of workers gathered to support the North in the American Civil War and to oppose the British government's intention to intervene on behalf of the slaveholding southern states— which for

Marx had a profound and far-reaching implication. The Italian radical Garibaldi was welcomed at mass meetings in London, and an insurrection in Poland was vigorously supported; all these meetings, furthermore, were organised by the London Trades Council who had worked with Marx and Engels over the years.

In September 1864 the same group of workers' leaders called for an international meeting, to promote solidarity across national frontiers and to ensure that the workers of different nations would not be played off against one another by the capitalists. Although he was not party to the founding of what would soon become the International Working Men's Association, Marx was invited to participate. He had not been particularly involved in the previous year or two, but Marx seized the opportunity because, as he put it, this time it was organised "by people who really count", that is, by workers' leaders — though those who attended the meeting were not all working class by any means, or all committed to the international workers' cause.

Asked to draw up its rules and principles, Marx had to be more nimble footed than ever before. Even those who had acknowledged his key role and asked him to take part were suspicious of socialism, and wholly unconvinced of the need for revolution. For the English trade union leaders, their target was to win the vote for all workers (see Paul Foot's wonderful *The Vote: How it Was Won and How it was Undermined*, London, 2005). Attending from France were delegates strongly influenced by Proudhon, Marx's old adversary. The Italians were dominated by Mazzini's radical nationalism.

This was an extraordinary political opportunity — to

win a dominant influence for revolutionary ideas among the leaders of the workers' movement — even though at this stage it seemed only a movement in embryo. Yet Marx's studies of the development of capitalism for *Capital* had reinforced his understanding of the way that the burgeoning of European capitalism was also a time in which the working class would grow in numbers and the conflicts between capital and labour would inescapably deepen. His account of the experience of workers' struggles in the *Address to the International* showed how that had developed since 1848. What emerged from that analysis was the absolutely central conviction that internationalism in the working class movement was, even at this stage, indispensable to the struggle for socialism.

There is, in the rules, a careful clarification by Marx that no single centralised rules would be applied on the different sections — but it was equally clear to both Marx and Engels that the need for a central and unified direction in the movement would very quickly become clear in the debates within the International. Indeed the opening statement to the new set of rules echoes that most central of all Marx's ideas:

"The emancipation of the working class must be conquered by the working classes themselves...the struggle for emancipation of the working classes means not a struggle for class privileges or monopolies, but for equal rights and duties, and the abolition of all class rule..." (David Fernbach [ed], Karl Marx, *The First International and After*, Harmondsworth, 1981, p82).

The *Address* stressed that the objective was "the conquest of political power by the working class" a phrase differently understood by the various participants. This left room for manoeuvre and debate. But when, a year later, some French delegates challenged Marx's right to be present, an English trade union delegate reminded them that "Citizen Marx has devoted all his life to the triumph of the working classes" and another demanded that they "let all those who have studied political economy from a working class standpoint come by all means to our Congresses" (quoted in Nimtz, p185).

The opposition to Marx came from the followers of Proudhon, the majority of whom were workers but not, by and large, in the major industries of the new capitalism. Their background was skilled craftwork, and they were still largely wedded to Proudhon's idea of creating mutual societies in a kind of parallel alternative to capitalism.[3] This was the very opposite of Marx's insistence on creating a revolutionary organisation of workers preparing to challenge bourgeois class power and construct a different order of society, in which the interests of the majority would prevail and profit would no longer be the driving force that shaped the whole organisation of society.

In Germany the battle was waged with the followers of Ferdinand Lassalle, and the formation of the Social Democratic Workers Party under Wilhelm Liebknecht was a major step forward for the "Marx party".

3: It is worth noting that Proudhon also argued that female labour was a "degeneration" and that the proper place of women was in the home. This position was opposed root and branch by Marx, and finally defeated.

★9:
A
NEW
POWER:
THE
PARIS
COMMUNE

In 1871 history would give dramatic shape to these debates. In July 1870 Louis Bonaparte (Napoleon III) of France allowed the Prussian leader Bismarck to provoke him into declaring war. By September Napoleon was a captive. In Paris the government declared a republic under a government of national defence; its resistance was short-lived, however, and by February 1871 a National Assembly was elected for the specific purpose of negotiating peace with newly unified Germany.

The government, under the reactionary Thiers, sat in Versailles away from Paris. The capital, under siege from the Prussians, was abandoned by the government and the rich. Only the National Guard, the militia, protected the city. When Thiers, increasingly fearful of the threat of an armed populace, attempted to seize the National Guard's cannons at Montmartre, the inhabitants of the capital resisted and declared the establishment of the Commune.

For the two months of its existence Marx was riveted,

fascinated by the Commune. His criticisms and condemnation of Louis Napoleon's Second Republic had been as fierce as his prediction of a new revolution in France was confident. To be truthful, these were not the best conditions for a workers' rising, after months of siege and scarcity. Marx feared too that the isolation of the Parisian workers would spell defeat unless they marched against Versailles. And he knew also that this insurrection would be unlikely to exhibit the ruthlessness of a bourgeois state — and that the class enemy would have no such compunction.

But in his inspiring analysis of the Commune, Marx sees a vision of workers' power, the problems it will face, the limits it must overcome and the creativity it can show in its building of a new and different kind of order. A new power was born in the Paris Commune in March of 1871. Marx was its passionate defender, irrespective of his earlier misgivings. Indeed Marx sent his son-in-law Paul Lafargue to Paris to work with the Communards.

What was new about the Commune? *The Civil War in France*, Marx's examination of the Paris events, answers that question for his own generation — and for those to come. "This was essentially a working class government...the political form at last discovered under which to work out the economical emancipation of labour."

Most importantly, it abolished the instruments of bourgeois domination — the standing army, replaced by a people's militia, an "armed people"; the institutions of bourgeois democracy replaced now by a direct democracy in which all delegates could be instantly removed from their positions and fresh elections called (a right reborn in the soviets of the Russian revolutions of 1905 and 1917) and would receive no privileges as a result of their political duties — "the public service had to be done at workmen's wages". This was a new state. The old one, resting always, as Lenin would say, "in the last instance on the violent repression of the majority", was replaced in Paris with a kind of rule that was neither separate from nor set above the majority but subject to it. This was the dictatorship of the proletariat as Marx had imagined it so much earlier.

In its bare two months of life, the Communards had insufficient time to enact a new order — to address the emancipation of women, to abolish exploitation, to create communal structures of social life. As Marx put it, "the Commune's greatest achievement was its very existence". And from it Marx drew perhaps his most far-reaching political conclusion:

"The working class cannot simply lay hold of the ready-made state machinery and wield it for its own purposes" (Karl Marx, *The Civil War in France*, in Fernbach, *Karl Marx*, p233).

The bourgeois state exists to defend and perpetuate the rule of the capitalist class; a society dedicated to the redistribution of wealth, to equality and an end to exploitation requires its own instrument of power, the workers' state. In Paris, in those two months, history had provided a glimpse of what that society might look like, how organs of workers' democracy could be built, and also the terrible price of defeat.

In the Assembly of the Commune, there were 17 members of the International (and only a minority of these were followers of Marx). The 92 members of the Assembly covered a broad spectrum of views and beyond the defence of the Commune and the condemnation of the reactionary Republic there was little clarity. Proudhon's followers were divided — there were even some who sat on their hands at Versailles throughout these events.

Others were followers of Blanqui and Michael Bakunin, the Russian anarchist who would dispute the legacy of the Commune with Marx and ultimately bring about the demise of this, the first International. Bakunin was an enthusiastic conspirator and a committed enemy of the state — but he was no friend of the working class. Indeed Bakunin argued that the working class should not organise, nor prepare its own assault on power — to do so would be a form of authoritarianism. Instead — and here was the irony — the attack on the state would be launched by secret conspiratorial cells, accountable to no one and never answerable to those it claimed to represent!

Most importantly, Bakunin challenged that most central and precious of all Marx's principles — *that the emancipation of the working class must be the act of the working class itself*. Bakunin, at the next Congress of the International, in 1872, attacked the idea of a centralised and disciplined organisation. Marx and Engels gave their answer in the most emphatic of terms: the International, they said, is "a mighty engine for revolution, and not a debating club...it is a society organised for struggle and not for fine theories" (quoted in Nimtz, p231).

The Commune had demonstrated the courage and creativity of the working class, it had provided a glimpse of a new socialist order and it had demonstrated beyond question the need to abolish the bourgeois state in order to achieve it, and in its defeat and the terrible revenge (tens of thousands of Communards were killed), by a terrified ruling class, had illustrated with blinding clarity the need for the International.

The Commune had fallen, Marx argued, "because there did not appear in all the centres, in Berlin, in Madrid, etc, the revolutionary movement corresponding to this supreme uprising of the Paris proletariat" (quoted in Nimtz, p231). The task for the future was to learn and to ensure that next time the revolt would be much wider.

The internal divisions between Bakunin and Marx clearly meant that this International could not be that instrument. It was Marx and Engels themselves who "put the beast out of its misery". By 1876 the International was officially no more.

Marx died in March 1883. Paradoxically his final years had been free of the financial pressures that had made his life with Jenny and his children so precarious. But while there were some comforts in his ageing, nothing could compensate for the death of his children and the demise of his Jenny two years earlier. Engels, of course, was at his deathbed, just as he had accompanied Marx on every step of their revolutionary road since their first meeting. Engels lived another 12 years, a time that he devoted to disseminating the work of his friend, collaborator and comrade. With characteristic self-deprecation, Engels declared that with Marx's death "mankind was shorter by a head". He went on to say of his old friend:

"Marx was before all else a revolutionist. His real mission in life was to contribute, in one way or another, to the overthrow of capitalist society and of the state institutions which it had brought into being, to contribute to the liberation of the modern proletariat... Fighting was his element. And he fought with a passion, a tenacity and a success such as few could rival" (available at www. marxists.org/archive/marx/works/1883/death/burial).

★10: MARX FOR OUR TIME

There are always those who chorus that "Marx has nothing to tell the 21st century". There have always been those who argued, at every stage, that these ideas had had their day — and it was past. The fall of "Communism" is held up as the definitive proof that Marx is redundant.

It's true that in 1989 the regimes of Eastern Europe fell in quick succession. They had called themselves socialist, yet what was exposed as they collapsed was that the working class did not control these societies nor did their interests determine how resources were allocated. On the contrary, that central idea of Marxism — that revolution is the self-emancipation of the working class — had been turned on its head, to justify grotesque and brutal tyrannies in which a small group of rulers served their own interests at the expense of the majority. In each of these states what came to prevail was the logic of capital — accumulation at any cost, competition between states; yet these are the defining features of capitalism, not socialism.

To understand the impulses and laws of motion that explain how capitalism works, we are driven time and again to return to Marx. The relentless pursuit of surplus value still overwhelms all other considerations, and the world is shaped, or rather misshapen, by the dominance of capital.

The appearance of the labour process changes, the bourgeoisie may dress in different clothing or live in different ways, workers may increasingly wear white coats or uniforms to replace the overalls, and the factories may hum where once they were deafening. But the relationship between those who own, control and administer society's wealth and resources, and those whose survival depends on the wages they are paid to produce the wealth, remains exactly as Marx described it. If anything, capitalism in our century looks more like Marx's picture of it than it did in his. The working class of South Korea alone is today bigger than that of the mid-Victorian world Marx knew. It is far easier to speak of a world working class today than it was in Marx's time.

Greenhouse gases, poisoned lakes, the desertified expanses of the world and the twisted empty monuments to earlier moments of industrialisation testify to the relentless transformation of the world even to the brink of destruction.

But Marx was concerned to understand capitalism and its brutalities not to make a moral critique, but to prepare for the emancipation of the working class. Just as capitalism recognised no boundaries or frontiers to its expansion, so the revolutionary movement of the working class must be international. Its organised strength would one day sweep away the structures of power and domination and bring about the death of the state itself; but that would not come automatically, but through the struggle of workers. And in the course of that struggle, not only would the power of capital be challenged and overcome, but a new society would be born in which the resources of mankind will be used to achieve human freedom.

The task was never more urgent than it is today.

A GUIDE TO READING

If you have been inspired to go on reading your way into Marx let me recommend:

Alex Callinicos, *The Revolutionary Ideas of Karl Marx* (Bookmarks, London, 2004). A comprehensive and accessible account of Marx's ideas to which I owe a great deal.

Karl Marx, *The Communist Manifesto*, with an introduction by Chris Harman (Bookmarks, London, 2005).

Karl Marx, *Selected Writings* (edited by David McLellan, Oxford University Press, Oxford, 2000).

Hal Draper, *Karl Marx's Theory of Revolution* (Monthly Review Press, New York, published in four volumes, 1978-90). Not for the faint-hearted, but a brilliantly clear exposition of Marx's ideas and the debates around them in four volumes.

August Nimtz, *Marx and Engels: Their Contribution to the Democratic Breakthrough* (SUNY Press, Albany, 2000). This is an academic study, but a fascinating one, of Marx and Engels' political activity.

John Bellamy Foster, *Marx's Ecology* (Monthly Review Press, New York, 2000). A demanding but brilliant look at the implications of Marxism for the ecological debate.

Frances Wheen, *Karl Marx* (Fourth Estate, London, 1999). An affectionate, well-written account of Marx as man and thinker.

The Marxist Internet Archive carries the vast majority of Marx's writings. Go to www.marxists.org

A Rebel's Guide to
LENIN

IAN BIRCHALL

The world today is very different from the one Lenin knew.
Yet if he came back to life Lenin would recognise some
things all too quickly – endless wars, the pillage of the
poor countries by the rich corporations, the corruption of
mainstream politicians.

This book offers an accessible introduction to Lenin, the
man, his ideas and their relevance to the 21st century.